Half a Decade in
My Labyrinth

TATIANA SPENCE

authorHOUSE®

AuthorHouse™
1663 Liberty Drive
Bloomington, IN 47403
www.authorhouse.com
Phone: 1 (800) 839-8640

Published by AuthorHouse   04/23/2015

ISBN: 978-1-5049-0816-0 (sc)
ISBN: 978-1-5049-0815-3 (e)

Library of Congress Control Number: 2015906559

Print information available on the last page.

This book is printed on acid-free paper.

Dedicated to everyone who believed in me, even when I stopped writing.

Dedicated to everyone who wanted to see me publish my first book.

Dedicated to everyone who walked in and out my life.

Dedicated to everyone who I shared a memory with.

Thank you

Contents

Taboo 1

I Am Not An Object 4

Dont' Forget I am Women 6

Turn 8

Smile Artist 9

Have You ? I know I Have. 11

Time Has Changed (Train Love) 12

Shadow Love 13

Black Rose..15

Let Us Shed Some Light Where
There Has Only Been Shade.......................17

Beautiful Deception 19

Expression 20

Identity Drift...23

I Never Understood, But All I know is 24

I've Seen Stars Fall..26

I'm Waiting on you (Lilly Pad) 28

This is a Subtle Whore.................................31

Troy 33

Voiceless Victim 35

Keep The Film Going (Make it look good)....37

Stars and the sky 39

I don't Care 40

Myles...41

He Is Love 43

Aspiration 45

Intimate, Intellectual, Education 47

Nude Eyes 49
Another Star 50
Experiment 52
No (date rape) 55
In Time 57
Silver Harp 59
Boy 60
Run Away Home 61
Trap House 63
Boom 64

Taboo

Love
Used in vain
Misconception
Conceived in the womb,
-to believe
Pure thoughts
When birthed from a non virgin
Can pure still exist
Monsters and murderous things
Are pulled into our world
From the non pure
Deception and spite
Are born from impurity
They live among us
We chose to believe,
Pure Love does exist
First mistake in deceiving yourself
Second,
Allowing yourself to relinquish all skepticism
Being pulled in
By this illusion you have created
Built from scratch
Imagination
Four walls that don't exist
You put them there
Four walls that don't exist
You built them here
To keep the Lies in as a Reality

While the truth locked out
Nightmare,
Living in a dream world
It's superficial
Believe it or not
When you get close up
Really look at the paint
Red ain't really red
Blue ain't really blue
That's when you get skeptic
Lying to yourself,
-Aint enough anymore
The cracks become open
The truth becomes the truth
The Lies become the betrayal
And you stopped believing
You know better
Don't lie to yourself
Live in a perfect perception
Create this memory
That doesn't exist
And think it's really there
It just makes it harder
To get back to reality
To realize the world ain't pure
Four walls that don't exist
You trapped yourself here
Four walls that don't exist

You will never see clear
Living in a dream world is fun
Until the truth sinks in
That's when you realize it's too late
You're mind polluted
Corrupted
That's when you have a choice
Decimate the world
Or Decimate you
That's why Love is Taboo

I Am Not An Object

I am not an object
I am human too
I feel and hurt just like you do
I am not an object for your use
A punching bag for your anger
Something to beat on,
-When you cannot get your way
I am a women
I demand Respect too
You cannot break my spirit
Unless I allow myself to be broken
You cannot make me bow to You
I am not a puppet for your muse
A doll at your disposal
Something to thrash against the wall!
And when I do not break!
And my body does not shatter!
Nor has my mind been manipulated!
I can still think for myself !
A heart is a heart
It is only an organ to live with
My love comes from my mind,
- and my mind is telling me
To love myself,
Respect myself,

And keep peace in myself,
-Do not let others disrupt my" Chi"
It is the fire in ourselves
We have yet learn to tame
To mold,
To control,
The flow of emotions
So until we learn the value of our women
We cannot love our women
Protect "our women"
When "we" being "men",
-Are disgusted by men who are predators.
When the men we are with are predators
-themselves in the making.
They forget to look in the mirrors
Ask themselves,
Am I the thing I am disgusted with ?
Have I become the man on the other side,
- of the mirror?
Did I miss the grass fading where it is no,
-longer greener on the other side?
So I speak again
I am not an object
I am human too
I feel and hurt just like you do
How do you not know our value
If you say we mean way more to you.

Dont' Forget I am Women

I am women
I am not part beast
yet I go on rampages
the ocean floor is calm one moment
and a storm arrives the next
i am angry
with you, with him,
-with the man to your left
i do not know his name
but he has stumbled into my path
he has provoked me !
Called me names which i am not !
shunned me !
Thrown me to the dogs for the kill
bloodshed is what they crave !
my blood, your blood
her's on your right
Do not belittle me
do not look down on me
I am BOLD i am strong, courageous
I can do what the next man can
We are equal
do not throw the shades of my skin

in my face
do not neglect me
because i am not in your norm
we shall conquer
this ignorance
that one alone can dominate
let us rise together
to your left, to your right,
All of us !
Stand Together
For We are Here !
don't forget we are capable of anything,
-you can do and more
don't forget we are women !

Turn

And when you have fallen
onto the hard dirt
and the thorns have scratched your skin
and your eyes no longer twinkle
your smile has faltered
allowing venom to pour into your soul
and black to pour out
when your eyes turn from brown to red
when the devil whispers for you to come near
hell cracks open beneath earths floors
the sky is magenta
our peoples tears are the color of blood
I will say out Satan!
Give me your hand friend
let me refill your heart with light
show you gods way
take the heaviness out of your heart
bring back your original spirit
protect you from the storm
walk together with me
let us heal your wounds
turn to heaven's gates
away from the cracks in the walls
ignore the whispering voices
pour in the sun
and let the moon within you glow
from the inside out

Smile Artist

They say a picture tells a thousand words
but what if i am the artist?
I got the paint
i paint the picture
the image
that you all see
does it really tell a thousand ?
or does it just let you see
-what I want you to see ?
Smile.
Broken Lines
Curved edges
turned into something more complex
To feel
And to be Felt
are two different things
If you paint the image,
-you gotta act like you own it.
Dont let the Scenery,
-Own you to express the exact vision
would be to tell a thousand words
rather we layer it with false perfection
Hoping that you never touch the paint before it dries
Never look closely to see between the lines

Never forget to blink
As the the artist begins to cry
And then we recollect ourselves
By then the canvas is done
and the damaged is already concealed in a portrait
And through wounded Art
The Artist Smiles

Have You ? I know I Have.

You ever love someone after Midnight ?
Wake up and still love them in the morning.
Get lost at sea and drown.
Yet find your way back to float in their love
Fall asleep in strong arms,
Under a shady tree
Watch the sunset,
-while smiling into big brown eyes
Have you ever gazed at someone
You never had to beg to listen
With open ears,
-With an understanding heart
Someone who time stops for,
-And feels like a century
Yet its only been five minutes
Someone who doesn't take your breathe away,
-But breathes with you.
Someone who smiles from hearing your laughter
Someone who takes pleasure in
seeing you happy all the time.
-Someone whose love knows no boundaries.
No time frame, no story line can capture
all the love you've saved for me.

Time Has Changed
(Train Love)

You were as beautiful as the stars
-in the sky years ago.
How you have aged lovely
Although you still look the same
With beauty skin deep
With a heart that has melted
-Lacking the touch of me
Your heart has grown fond of my absence
How you have gained so much wisdom
A love that was drowned in the river
Saved?
Impossible.
But time has changed
We have changed
Is it possible to grow together?
Or will be deceived by each other?
At the end of this train ride
Will it just be a dream
As the train comes to a stop
I reach for you....
And thats all I remember

Shadow Love

Your love is so beautiful,
-but yet you stand in the shade
Leaving me in the spotlight
digging me a grave
your love is so abstract
and my heart is so full
but how can we compare
when we don't add up
how can we be a pair
when we don't match up

Loving your shadows,
-is not what i had in mind
seeing us from your point of view
-I've desperately tried
and its like making a wish,
-in a empty wishing well
hoping it would turn out right,
-and it would be all well

turning my love into a different scenery
hoping it would be okay with me
investing my time in creating visions
when your love is just a mystery to me

And I'm Done,

But Before i walk away from this,
-shadow love
i put this dove in a box
say farewell to my beloved
its like it never happened,
-that's what you call a shadow love

Black Rose

As lovely as you've blossomed
You're a black rose
With your hidden thorns
Unforeseen scratch marks
Black petals covered in red dew
But green stems,
- with no thorns
Be warned of the obvious danger
Lurking
creeping up
Don't pick the flower
Don't inhale its exquisite sent
Luring you in
Blindly by its persuasion
Deceiving yourself of clear deception
And yet the rose cuts you
Silently. In the middle of the night
Like a nightmare
Locked in the dream world
As you feel your blood pour black
-All over the floor
And its not a dream
But it feels like one

But you're not screaming
Engulfed by the black roses
That's when you know you can't love anymore
Stolen shadows
Misplaced soul
Cold blooded
And the twinkle in your eye turns gray
Making the concept of loving foreign
Leaving a tint of black that covers your soul
Oh, the grey got you too
Desirable. Lovely blacks rose
Oh, how you've become one too

Let Us Shed Some Light Where There Has Only Been Shade

Did you forget?
Who believed in your dreams,
-when you forgot to believe in yourself
when you were giving up your goals
And I was fighting your battles
when making it to the finish line,
-became a challenge
I helped you crossed it
I helped you shed some light,
-where there has only been shade

Remember those times you cried
The Nights were dark and lonely
The stars had ran away
And the clouds had vanished from sight,
-no longer hiding you
But I stayed
I Stayed where there has only been shade

Time flies when you're an acrobat
And when i join you on the trampoline
I can fly too
Forgetting all the bitterness of the world
Be Free
Touch the sky

And feel a little bit higher
And when the shade doesn't block the sun
And i step from under the tree
Off the trampoline i go!
Landing with a thud
Just a peek outside of are umbrella tree
I see, what the unconscious knew,
-all along

Reality it seems never fails
Talk about don't tell lies
Don't keep secrets
But you kept one

And now it festers in that old tree
I step away from the tree
and a root reaches out!
Wrapping around my leg
desperately trying to pull me in
I fall backwards
Come says the tree
Stay says the tree
I'm sorry

I close my eyes
Concentrating on the light
Wiping the sympathy out my heart
The tree roots turn to ash
And the tree is engulfed into the ground.

Beautiful Deception

your eyes
oh so lovely
your lips just the right amount
of shine
to pull me in
to lower me with your hints
your lovely words
your poison
on the tip of my tongue
like sweet venom,
in disguise
you are a traitor
i am your prisoner
but i don't know that
you feed me to the sharks
you take away my soul
the very thing i gave you to safe keep
you lock my most prize possession to you,
- in a jar
my best organ
covered in blood
after you slowly dragged it out of me
and as you carved that knife in through the front
i never once flinched as the blade touched my skin
you were amazing
Even Till' the very end
I still never knew
that's what you call a beautiful Deception

Expression

i wanted to express myself
open to someone
share how i felt from my heart
have someone listen and understand
not brush me off into the wind
i wanted to express myself
to be heard and understood
to feel the love and compassion
-every human being needs to survive
but i won't bore anyone
anyone with my sad tails
my battered eyes
my wounded ribs
have been bruised again
yet this rib cage remains
the frame around my heart
my skull that's tattered
worn thin, from impact
from devastation
will soon collapse inwards
this skull of mines holds eyes
eyes that burn my skull
and burn my mind
but mind is abstract

so how can something abstract hurt ?
because we make it hurt
it is Love
It is Expression
I wanted to express myself
to anyone who's willing to listen
Not Really,; only a few in particular
i wanted to climb a tree
and fall at the same paste,
-as a leaf
and when i hit the ground
by then i have turned brown
maybe orange or a reddish color
but either way i have wilted
faded away out of existence
just like that leaf
that fell from the tree
That is Expression;,
-A girl crying to be heard
screaming to be heard
to be acknowledged
but she has slowly given up
given up trying to reach out
out to the outside world
she slowly fester's away,

from the inside out
but you can't see it, why ?
Because it is abstract
She is slowly Becoming abstract herself
detached from the world
cut off from reality
Forgetting her delusion is a delusion,
-since it has become her reality
that is a form of Expression.

Identity Drift

You were once a undesirable,
-to others
but now you grew up
you didn't change
you stop being a caterpillar
walked into the light of fame
became a butterfly
you stopped standing in the shade
people started to know your name
You Never Turned Hollywood
You Remembered Everybody's Names
Even those who forgot you
Always remember to turn the other cheek
i use to think getting even was right
but all it does is make you weak
Being the better person does show i've evolved
doesn't mean that i'm weak
only difference is,
- i've changed from simple minded
to a complex view.
Meaning it takes a whole lot more to get to me,
-then to get to you.
My Perception Now and Then Has Shift
That's what you call an identity drift

I Never Understood,
But All I know is

I never understood why the sky
held in all it's emotions
sighed out a blast of tears
filling the world with despair
sadness and the blues
i never knew why i took out my umbrella
to ignore the sky's pain
to turn away from a friend
who is abstract
but still brings sunshine to my day
-on happy days
And when it roared to be heard
we ran away
all of us
frolicking to houses and stores
something that could separate us
and when lightning struck
it scared us even more
sending us back closing curtains
locking doors
running to stores to take food for ourselves
how selfish we are
all the sky wanted was a moment of our time
some attention from the closest thing to it
us human beings

so it wept and it wept
until one day it decided
it wasn't gonna cry anymore
the clouds came and brought foggy days
to hold back most of the tears
but all i know is the sky still cries
a voice wanting to be heard
misunderstood
pushed out and ignored
We have too much love
to throw away
and yet we throw none to the sky
why is that ?
Have we forgotten what the sky has done for us ?
What have we done for the sky
who hums silent blues
to calm it's heart
and keep it's mind at bay
But all i know is,
we will make it greener on the other side some day.

I've Seen Stars Fall

I've seen stars fall
paint drip off the wall
little girls sit in corners
and cry
shadows creeping up
gravity falling on mama's back
my eyes rolling back
dreaming off
green grass
blue skies
better days will come to light
tears drip from everywhere
my eyes, my back, my palms
and secretly mama's eyes
love and to be cherished
and valued
is something we long for
yet we fear
for resentment
of being let go
forgotten lost
turning to hopelessness
and faded into an eternal dark whole
I've seen stars cross the sky
I've seen them drip like rain drops
falling out of the sky

what's that knocking?
i don't know
but it's something we all fear
to be inhaled like a bundle of joy
and exhaled like waste
to exist in one instant
and vanish like poof
in another
i long for what you long for
to hold a place in a place
where burden is not herd off
rain does not fall from my body
and my heart
is secured on a pillow
or cushion
or even your arms
if not mama's
where i will always
feel wanted and belong

I'm Waiting on you (Lilly Pad)

your like a lilly
floating on a pond baby
i cant reach you
i cant hold you
and the waters arctic
baby it's cold out here without you
and im trying to reach you before i freeze
but this ice is creeping on me
your like a lilly
floating on the wind
i can't smell your aroma
you're too far
from my arms
i can't grasp your waist
i cant reach you in time
it's almost noon
and it's gonna rain soon
i don't have time baby
i need to reach you now
your soul is drifting
in and out
-like a faded memory
Like a canvas with a running painting
you gonna run from me baby?
what are you scared of?
is it fear ?

eating you alive?
has that soft spot been infected?
with something
other than love
has graced the presence
of that soft tissue over your heart
you're like a lily baby
and i'm still trying to reach you
the rain is drizzling down now
it's tapping on the top of your
-lilly pad,
its pouring now
and i can't see you on the surface
your eyes baby i can't see you anymore
it's rain all over my body
i need you here
your gone in the wind
your drowning?
i hear it
i hear you,
-come back !
i see this lilly sinking
you're under the surface now
i'm chasing you
but i'm freezing under water baby
trying to reach you

to hold you once more...
the frost consuming my body
the temperature continues to drop
my hair now white as snow
your drowning
and i can't reach you
but i'm not ready to let go
and then i barely touch your lilly pad
deprive of oxygen and heat
i enter a coma
instantly
followed by sudden death
trying to reach you
to hold you
to feel your body
through the rain and wind
again
just to smell your aroma
my sweet sweet dear Lilly Pad

This is a Subtle Whore

Can it be?
But a star in the clouds has fallen
The once tight room
Is now filled with shattered glass
And there it lays all the lies
They surround me

I dear breathe another breath
This is fortune?
Indeed I am fortunate to have Iago
But unfortunate for the news he brings me
These graves you dig are you not ashamed of?
Can you not admit what you are?
& what you have done?

Away with your soul
Your face is no longer welcome
Your hand to my heart
Your chest to mine
You are not of my kind
And therefore I am not to mingle with you anymore

Games?
Is this what this is to you?
I am no arcade of your choice
This is not a walk in the park!
I cannot say

The moon it curves
The path you travel is not so straight
Neither may I say faithful
But it burns me with a million stars
For you to burn me
I am not the one
You are not the one
There will be none of this

A white horse saw more than me
An Irish man has more gold than me
Was our marriage a shame to you?
And a waste for me?

"You are a subtle whore,
A closet locked with a key and villous secret:
And yet she'll kneel and pray; I have seen her do 't"
As if the gods will save you

You have no place with god
You have no place with me
Be gone with you
You leave bitter yet sweet
-sorrow in my soul.

Troy

For all the thoughts I gave of you
For every moment, I fought for you
I broke everything I stood for
I went out of my way
Time and time again.
And you didn't for me.

Colors I saw weren't for me
They were for you
They were for our little star
You made me smile
You lighted up my world.
And I adored you

I fought to stay in
I fought to keep them out
I looked for any battle
To keep you mine
I blocked out all the sounds
All the voices that reached me

The moon and the stars I reached for you
I did it all for you
I became the opposite
-of what you saw me to be
I became a heart
And I had a little heart in me.

And it hit me
I was always there
You were always there
And you kept leaving the whole time
And I kept chasing after you
In a dream and out
Me and my little heart kept chasing about

You did something
You got rid of my little heart
I realize I was my own happiness the whole time
I made me laugh, me smile
Not you, never you
And now I knew.
What I had to do
Leave for good

Voiceless Victim

He touched her
He ruined a part of her mind
Twisted and disgusted
He took some of her space
He violated her
Without a second thought
He messed up one little girl
He put a hand on her
He corrupted her spirit
He faded her smile
A dent in her independence
A little fear in her heart
Paranoia lurks in her bones
She freezes at the memory
She freezes at the crime scene
Voiceless victim she is
Voice of anger she shouted
No one herd besides her attacker
No one knows of this voiceless victim
And now she lives with a little fear
-in her heart
That another predator
Will prey on her
Because she is young
She is vulnerable
Only herself

Can free her from bondage
Of this heavy note put on her heart
Speak up said the birds
Tell your story
Because there are many like you
His hand slid a long so quickly
His mind in a wrong world
The image of the girl
Reflected in the mirror
It's a little bit faded
The mirror is worn
Cracks along the edges
But she never forgot the story
The details to it all
All revolving around the word "He"
Guess what
"That was me"

Keep The Film Going
(Make it look good)

We gotta make us look good
make it look like a movie
were the main stars
let's show them who we are
let's put on a good show
keep the crowd going
show them what they don't want
let them see what we want
make it look beautiful
hold my hand smile
wave to everyone
let them know how happy we are
Let them wait for our fall
which they can't see
but it's coming
are we running out of film?
are there no more scripts ?
We have to keep rehearsing
because as soon as we step out
into daylight
into the spotlight
were the main attraction
so make it look good
keep the film going

we have a huge audience
let's give them something to cheer for
how about we work out
the mistakes
rewrite the future script
give them something to cheer for
give them everlasting love.
To keep the film going
give them something that's real
make it look good
let our love touch your souls
engulf the audience
there is no end to us
so will keep the film going
we don't have to make it look good

Stars and the sky

remember when,
we looked at the stars,
and the sky,
and magic wishes,
took us to another place,
in time,
trees moved closer,
to river banks,
night fall took forever
and when the moon arrived,
I would stare up
it would look back
watching over
me,
you,
preserving our dreams
fairytale magic
in a white snowball
nobody could steal,
are magic dust,
to break it,
stop believing
the sky would fall upon us
the stars would cascade,
to the earth,
and the magical dust
would turn to snow
a moonlight explosion

I don't Care

Nobody is you
don't let them
let you
make yourself
Feel
When you don't have to
because,
If you don't need to,
-care
Emotions,
shouldn't be there
anywhere
involved
in things
That don't matter

Myles

He is movement
In and out my arms
He is a tidal wave,
- that ripples in my heart
His pulse is my pulse
He's not a mystery
Nor a solved puzzle
He is exactly how I want him
The way he wants himself
Warm in my arms
Embraced fully in my heart
Full big eyes,
- lost in mine
Lost in each other
All we have
Is enough
We can take the world
Get lost in time
Future, past, present
Presently together
Futurely forever
My every being
Casted over
Spell bound
Time testing me

Faith sending me
My heart is telling me more
More, More More
Wrapped in his blankets
Asleep on his chest
Locks and keys
Keys and locks
My heart is cracked
And so is yours
But the cracks keep us,
- open to each other
Keep us flowing
Exploring
One New memory at a time.

He Is Love

I wanted him
But it wasn't just 'x'
I wanted his soul
In my arms
His all
His love
His lips
Eyes
Belove beloved
I wanted him all for myself
Selfish
Tears poured on me
His tears
Not mine
Nails gashed into his back
I wanted him in his most naked form
To watch blood shed
To be all
I longed an infinite love
For fear it shall disappear
Just as it came
I refrain from the simple use of language
Three words not spoken
Foolish
Only a child would say it

For they not know
A love is more complex,
- than simple
Or rather we make it complex
To avoid the simplicity,
- Of falling in love
Instead one can only dream
Of those three words
Tucked away from her lips
One can only look into his eyes
Have him look back at her
Let the connect of two eyes,
- be all the love they need,
To simply just be.

Aspiration

knowing is key
Grasping is the logical answer
when,
only time will tell
don't fuss
don't fight
dont push
haste will lead you,
-astray
stand steadfast
hold on to your soul
For that is where,
-the art of creativity
sprung from
the inspiration
within you
should live on
outside you
your achievements
engraved into the earth's,
-surface,
leave your mark
as an expression

Of your character
impression
founded upon
living hearts
sculpted new talents
creating sequels,
-to your soul
Other Soul's aspiring to be like you

Intimate, Intellectual, Education

I wanna dive into your body
Through your mind
Touch places,
That have never been explored
Take you to another galaxy
Wrap your waist around my mind
Then we can discuss circumferences
Have you climax to new thoughts
Shout ideas
That have you speaking in,
-new perceptions
Create theories that are testable
Results,
Multiple conclusions
Give you an opportunity
To rethink the situation
Evaluate the heat of the moment
Substitute X with him
And Y with you
Calculate possible errors
That means a child in you
Unplanned
Then we gotta go back

Erase
Use are predicament as a base
To solve the equation
A problem
Outcome unaccounted for
A variable that was always a possibility
constantly overlooked
Young women in the making
Don't forget the best form of protection
It isn't a condom
Its a womens education

Nude Eyes

turned heads
open eyes
no tears
I am a conquer
Ask me
A million questions
My Life story
Don't read my eyes
You wont find
What your looking for
My Lips
They Speak to you
I tremble
At the thought
Of revealing myself

Another Star

seen stars fall
paint drip off the wall
little girls sit in corners
and cry
shadows creeping up
gravity falling on mama's back
my eyes rolling back
dreaming off
green grass
blue skies
better days will come to light
tears drip from everywhere
my eyes, my back, my palms
and secretly mama's eyes
love and to be cherished
and valued
is something we long for
yet we fear
for resentment
of being let go
forgotten lost
turning to hopelessness
and fading into an eternal dark whole
i've seen stars cross the sky
i've seen them drip like rain drops
falling out of the sky

what's that knocking?
i don't know
but it's something we all fear
to be inhaled like a bundle of joy
and exhaled like waste
to exist in one instant
and vanish like poof
in another
i long for what you long for
to hold a place in a place
where burden is not herd off
rain does not fall from my body
and my heart
is secured on a pillow
or cushion
or even your arms
if not mama's
where i will always
feel wanted and belong

Experiment

We are friends
We are integrated
We hug, we show compassion
But when my color seeps onto,
-your clothes,
-into your pores
-making your soul,
-just a little darker
you flinch of the thought
of being me
of being closer to my shade
Your soul and my soul
We are both good people
Why is it wrong to look like me
Why is it heartbreaking
To see the mirror
To see yourself as me
But to still be just you
If your shade would be
-the same as mine
We would be no different
Things would not change much
Is my skin not pretty enough?
Is my complexion not well toned?
Am I an my color inferior?
Is my spirits complexion
Is your skin so crystal clear
That my beautiful dirt brown

-color
Cannot shine too?
That you would rather
Buy your freedom
From the bondage of a skin
As if it was a disease
A medical condition
That you will suffer from
As if we should pity you
For being forced to be
Something you're not
sad
"You are who you say
you are"
You will always be you
no matter the skin
-you're in
It is your mentality that,
-makes you think
that we
Are less beautiful than you
That you would feel
Less beautiful in my skin
My skin is beautiful
My skin is comfy
Just as I am me

You will always be you
No matter the color,
-of your skin
Money can never
-buy the real you
that is the mentality
you should have
priceless
we are all priceless

No (date rape)

He's a nice guy in public
But behind close doors
He's trying
To loosen you up
Relinquish all rights
Submit to his command
Comply with his wishes
You say no
He hears try again
It's code for yes
Make another advance
Use a little more force
Grab and pull her
When she gets up
Follow her
Try again
A stern no becomes weaken
You think she's caving
Continue repeated advances
Forcing your way some more
Until she submits
At the cost of avoiding discomfort
While entertaining it
In the presences of a "nice guy"
Not so nice anymore
Men in the making forget

Women think with their mouths
Therefore when she speaks no
-listen
Do not reinterpret the situation
To fit what your ears desire
Rather hear what is spoken
Take note, and respond accurately
In your decisions
No matter what your body says
What hers says
Hear her lips
No means no
Yes means yes
Do not momentarily forget
Basic communication skills
Because not all women hush
Some will bark
And the moment they do
You've traded basic listening skills
Never applied
For fours walls
A cell

In Time

See the love has to fade
All these shades and heels
New keys
Occupy me
Your love
Denied me
These clothes kept warm
A love that will not love
Condemned to circles
Distant lovers
Connected mind
Felt vibes
Increasing time
Maximizing trust
Yet never together
Maybe not in this lifetime
But the next
You'll abandon my love
Or I'll jump
Hanging love
Clinging in unison
Longing to unite

Avoiding the commit
Hearts safe at bay
Far from shallow waters
Sinking sand
Not in water
But I still drown in your love
Not suffocating
Engulfed by your aroma

Silver Harp

Silver Harp
Plays a tune
Irregular vibe
Tap dancing in my shoes
Yet soft on my heart
Like a cold bathe
To keep me lively
Remind me
Why I play a tune
So simple
Yet hypnotizing
Aware of these chains
Prisoner I am not
Captor I am
My own hostage
Dancing in my chains
For fear of letting the music stop
Dreading what will come next

Boy

I love you said that boy
Your wild hair
Odd behavior
Bitter taste in men
Sweet heart
Compassionate human being
Thrills of life
Never running
Always living
Weather on the edge
Or at the core
Dancing on tables
Sweeping floors
Your no Cinderella
No saint
But you're an angel
Your no Cruella De Vil
But you've got heart
I've adorn you for some time
Just as you have adorn me
But waters we tremble on
Are a delicate matter
Tap dancing
In the same room as you
Is Enough to create friction
Before the clock strikes
You have disappeared once more
Just as I elope again

Run Away Home

you think it doesn't exist
but it does
it lurks in you
the containment
longing to be released
free
to live all your imagination
desires
At any cost
hurting yourself
having a dream realized
The farther I fly
the higher i feel
wider my smile
closer the clouds become
to my face
Face it
There's love in me
who am i willing to give it to
Run with my love
no longer caring
where it may fall

please I know
You're not living
until you break all
Contradict
Be Young
Don't ever
Let them
Take you
please

Trap House

Killing
she's a beauty
In here
Diminishing herself
forgetting the struggle
Making a name
Infamous
Getting that bread
Any means necessary
Don't fight the system
work with it
bondage and shackles
She knows not
Undercover
deluding herself
She's crack

Boom

You ever had one thing
And got the other
Thought you had something
But you had another
Saw the world opened up
But missed the part where you were,
- sinking
Thought you were soaring high
But deep down you were crashing
Felt like you had it all
But it mysteriously somehow,
-vanished
Leaving you to wonder
What is the definition of blind
How could you wake up
Be aware of today's day
But not know the actual events
Not being able to account for
The actual story
Your life's climax
Then downfall
The bridges of in between
Misguided
Inactive intuition
Never taking action

Leaving it to common sense
Which is not so common
To take charge
Just when we think,
We are in the right
We are not
Things change
Just like the weather
While we blindly walk to tomorrow
Let us improvise are next move
The next plan

Printed in the United States
By Bookmasters